I.O. - I.O.

Julian H. Hyman

Bloomington, IN 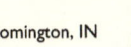  Milton Keynes, UK

AuthorHouse™
1663 Liberty Drive, Suite 200
Bloomington, IN 47403
www.authorhouse.com
Phone: 1-800-839-8640

AuthorHouse™ UK Ltd.
500 Avebury Boulevard
Central Milton Keynes, MK9 2BE
www.authorhouse.co.uk
Phone: 08001974150

First published by AuthorHouse 2/15/2007

ISBN: 978-1-4259-7777-1 (sc)
ISBN: 978-1-4259-7778-8 (hc)

Library of Congress Control Number: 2006910270

Printed in the United States of America
Bloomington, Indiana

This book is printed on acid-free paper.

THIS BOOK IS DEDICATED TO

Paulyne Ruttenberg Hyman, my wife for over one half century –
mother of our two wonderful children, helpmate – human being.

I..H. (Bud) Hammerman, II longtime friend – college roommate
– supporter – philanthropist – human being.

Contents

The foundation of the following treatis is based on (I.O.-I.O.) intuition-observation-imagination-opinion.

It is my conviction that external controls can be involved in some of our lines of thoughts and in conclusions reached. We are being coached and perhaps manipulated. Many seemingly accidental discoveries are not accidents.

I.O.-I.O. is an extensive report of the world we are thrust into when we are born. It offers solutions to some of the problems and solicits aid in the making of necessary corrections.

Julian Hyman

"Imagination is more important than knowledge; it is the gateway of progress and the preview of coming attractions."

Albert Einstein

"Never believe that a few caring people can't change the world for, indeed, that's all whoever have."

Margaret Mead

When the time comes for new knowledge to become available, it will not be confined to a single source, but will be scattered as seeds over the entire earth.

If the desire is strong enough, and if the body responds, it will happen.

Today's science fiction is a root of tomorrow's history.

Nothing is forever, as it had been it need not be, and it will not be.

If this book stimulates thought, it has served its purpose.

SYSTEMS

A major design of nature is the system, cause and effect. Machines are systems. Galaxies are systems. Chemical compounds are systems. Life itself is a system.

Systematic principles go from simple to extremely complex. All are based on cause and effect, using fixed precepts.

Examine the world in which we live. We are looking at organized infrastructures. Were they a hit, miss, random occurrence or was intelligence involved in their creation?

YOUR DECISION

A decision needs to be made on the flight of spaceship "Planet Earth." Did the human race arise and flourish because Earth was a prize, it had all the elements for life to flourish, or was Earth reconditioned adding additional elements needed to maintain a long line of generations of life-bearing entities?

Some of the things Earth has that makes it so hospitable.

1. A low range of temperature gradients. The rotation of the earth exposes its entire surface to sunlight. The angle of the axis of Earth's rotation is a 23½° tilt from the sun, providing equal seasons on both hemispheres of Earth, again equalizing temperature.

    Variable cloud cover also helps moderate temperature over Earth's surface.

2. The Earth's trip around the sun is a relatively short 365 days which also holds down temperature differentiation.

3. The surface of the Earth is two-thirds water, one-third land. This is sufficient for widespread water fall over the land. Rain not only promotes life but cleanses the atmosphere. Water is the root of life on this planet.

4. A gaseous envelope surrounds the Earth, 78% nitrogen, 21% oxygen; ideal for oxygen dependent life forms. The supply of it is balanced between plants and animals. Animals inhale oxygen and exhale carbon dioxide. Plants do the reverse a balanced system.

5. Slopes, hills, and mountains join with gravity to create waterways for the return of rain to the oceans. This completes the plan for a successful watering system.

6. Weather caused by a flow of air over the surface of the planet, initiated by the rotation of the planet, seasons, heating and cooling of the air, water, and surface by the changing effects of the sun's rays.

7. The interplay of these elements creates air mass differentials conducive to cloud formation, or the contrary. Temperature variants create areas of varying air pressure with resultant interplay of pressure differences, producing weather we live in.

8. Gender, the long voyage requires steady, constant life replacement. The continuous renewal of the same DNA creates a buildup of defects a dead end. The need is for a constant mix of DNA with each generation. Nature solves the problem by requiring two entities for reproduction in its species of plants and animals.

9. Gravity, strong enough to maintain the volume of Earth's gaseous envelope, preventing leakage into space.

10. A layer of ozone in the upper atmosphere shelters life on Earth from harmful sun radiation. It shrinks and expands. There is a system in its operation.

There are many other systems on Earth that benefit the continuity of life, diffuse, interactive, and complicated.

THE FERTILE EARTH

You reside on a modest sized planet in a system that nurtures you throughout your life, the generations, and our era.

The solar system of Earth since its inception has already traveled a huge distance. The distance to its allocated working area is mammoth. Human passengers on board are on an assignment.

This planet, this laboratory, is brimming with life. Try doing a summation of the living species existing on Earth at the same time; there are animals, birds, marine life, insects, reptiles, worms, etc.; flying, crawling, running, walking, jumping, slithering, swimming, floating, hopping, digging, climbing; sized from microscopic to huge.

How many billions of living creatures co-exist on this planet, benefiting from the presence of each other and at the same time struggling to maintain their own presence? All are going through the processes of birth, growth, maturity, mating, reproduction, decline, and death.

THE DESIGN

The surface of the Earth is broken into huge, irregular continental plates that float on a molten base of magma. Over millions of years, these continents have gradually shifted positions. This change stabilizes the rotation of the Earth, much as lead plugs are utilized to balance tires.

Planted in the outer layers of the Earth are pockets of petroleum, gases, elements, chemical compounds, coal, etc.

This applies to the entire surface of the world. When supplies are exhausted from the one-third land, there is still two-thirds to be recovered from under the water surfaces. Technology will be developed to allow humankind to drill and mine, neutralizing the tremendous pressure of the air and water above.

Lower stage presences act in concert with middle-stage life as operating machines, scavengers, and regulators. There is a strong symbiotic relationship in life forms.

THE FOUNDATION OF IT ALL

Fact 1 -   Life has existed on Earth for millions of years.

Fact 2 -   Originally, the Earth was barren. Changes progressed over the years. Early life forms were ruggedly constructed and mentally lacked the capacity for innovation.

Fact 3 -   In recent times, humankind appeared on Earth. Their power to innovate gave them dominion over other life forms.

Fact 4 -   Humankind possesses an emotional instability that can irrationally take control of individuals and nations.

Fact 5 -   The human machine is also endowed with a system of common sense; a counter balance to those emotions.

Fact 6 -   The emotional system and the common sense system are of approximately equal strength. They are in perpetual conflict.

Fact 7 -   You can influence your fate, but you are not the master of it.

PROBLEMS - SOLUTIONS

Humankind are on a path leading to the colonization of the solar system. We have taken our first stumbling steps into space.

As with any endeavor, there is good and bad. To colonize another planet, the same conditions humans live under on their home planet would be needed, and include water, oxygen, gravity, heat, cooling, waste disposal, communications, food, clothing, a medical environment, equipment, machinery, housing, entertainment, companionship, research facilities, local transportation, fuel, etc. A resupply program from Earth is essential.

The provisioning requirements are huge. Our present rocket propulsion engines are very primitive and wasteful. We will gradually improve the designs.

The practical way to use present knowledge is to substitute robots without the needed human logistics. This we are now doing.

A major limitation of our robotic machines is the inability of their repairing and replacing themselves. This problem will be addressed; ultimately robots will become very sophisticated and self-sufficient.

OUR MOON

The moon is a friend, present even when obscured by clouds or by its near invisibility in its smallest phases. It reflects the sun's rays, helping to illuminate the night. It tugs and pushes on the oceans, generating the tides. It has served as an ancient calendar. It has many advantages.

Earth's satellite will one day be Earth's terminal for space travel. Being airless, it will not broadcast the sounds of arrivals and departures. Being of low gravity, it will not require as much power to depart or to brake on arrival. Being a good distance from Earth makes it more secure to police against smuggling, terrorism, crime, and undesirable aliens. It is ideal for clearing government regulations for health checks and decontamination of arriving passengers and freight.

Interplanetary travel will involve dealing with strange diseases and strange creatures. There will be import and export controls, collections of duties, quarantine, etc. The isolation of the moon makes it ideal for controlled re-entry.

One defect is the necessity of transporting supplies, personnel, freight, and passengers to and from the Earth. The saving grace would be that by the time it will be needed, technology will have taken a great leap forward, minimizing the drawbacks.

BLACK HOLES

$$E = mc^2 \quad M = \frac{E}{C^2}$$

Conversion of energy to mass involves enormous forces, but as shown above, it is mathematically possible.

If the universes are unceasingly spewing energy, what would be the eventual effect on the total existence of mass?

Under the postulate that everything is a system, it is reasonable to expect a method of converting energy back into mass. Black holes perform that function.

They suck in all energy, including light. There are considerably more black holes than we have so far discovered.

If black holes convert energy into matter, what happens to the matter that is created? What about those large, gaseous clouds in space?

The universes themselves are machines. As we learn more about space, it will become apparent that existence is circular. Each occurrence is tied in partnership with other happenings. A unified field does exist.

CAN IT BE?

In space, there is a relationship between various bodies. There is an interplay between the physical characteristics of each galaxy through diverse systems.

Black holes perform an important function to other spatial existences, much as kidneys in the human system perform a vital function to the entire human body.

Space is inundated with celestial bodies, all in motion. Collisions occur between them. But there is still a degree of security in their orbits. Think of a pool of water, undisturbed by moving exterior influences. Drop a quantity of small floating objects into the pool. After they settle down on the undisturbed surface, they assume equilibrium of space to each other. What forces establish that equilibrium? Obviously, a similar force also exists in space.

THE HUMAN MACHINE

All living things are machines; every organ in your body has or had a purpose. Every organ contributes to the smooth function of the system of life. You exist utilizing and recycling the elements of your environment.

In the design of humankind, engineering principles have been used to guarantee quality and to produce lightweight and maximum strength, hinged joints, cushioning, and lubricating, as in spinal discs, cantilevered and arched bones, and mobility in limbs, eyes, neck, feet, hands and body. There are tears to wash the eyes, automatic blinking to wipe them; phlegm to clear the breathing passages; wax and hairs to protect the ears against invasion; hair in the nostrils; perspiration to cool the body; lymph to deliver nutrients and sweep out waste from the entire body; switched electrical circuits throughout the body; protective emotional reactions; reproductive drives; automatic repair of damaged tissue; automatic sneezing to clear the nostrils; coughing to clear the air passages; automatic finger- and toenail regrowth; automatic broken bone mending; automatic shifts from stage to stage of life; growth and decline. These are only a sample.

The human structure embodies numerous other involuntary systems — lungs spontaneously inhaling, exhaling air, heart rhythmically pumping blood, digestive system releasing chemicals when food is ingested, walls in motion to propel and process eaten food, etc.

A built-in calendar initiates stages of your development crawling, walking, talking, teething, puberty, mental maturing, menopause, followed by a steady decline in health until death.

THERE IS A COMMON PLATFORM

There is a common platform utilized in the design of Earth's life forms.

1. All consume nourishment.

2. It is digested.

3. Unusable waste is eliminated.

4. Most life forms utilize water.

5. There is an internal circulatory system.

6. There is a reproductive system.

7. All categories have the ability of motion and perception.

8. All have defensive systems.

9. All age.

10. All consume and are consumed.

IT CAN BE

There are various planes of existence, with their own laws of behavior, controlling life forms. The living creatures of various planes of existence cannot enter specific other planes. To do so would be suicide. The solution is the use of substitutes or adapters.

In our case, we revert to various machines to travel to other space bodies. We remotely control our exploring machines, or try to.

Humans are also machines that can be remotely controlled through emotions. Is there not a logical question? If such controls exist, why aren't they being used? Or perhaps they are.

You are very much at home on parts of the Earth. You are matched to the local environment. Move you to other environments and you will require encapsulation plus tools.

MACHINES

Living machines on Earth are exquisitely designed. Compare your body designs to the machines designed by humans themselves. Both are similar in basic conception but greatly unequal in quality.

	THE DESIGN OF YOUR BODY	HUMAN MADE MACHINES
Framework	Stiff bones, flexible muscles and tendons protect inner structure and maintain exterior shape. Bones are internal.	Stiff metal or plastic structures establishing internal structure and exterior shape.
Appendages	Jointed bone structures moved by the contraction or extension of muscles.	Wheels, rods or track coordinated with gears, hydraulics, cables, wires, electrical circuitry, chemical activity.
Cushioning	Cellular tissue, fat, muscle	Springs, flexible rods, sponge, plastics, air, rubber, hydraulics.
Nourishment	Tissue chemically converted to heat, energy, and basic chemicals through chemical interaction carried through pipes in a fluid propelled by a muscular heart pump.	Oil, hydrogen gas, propane, sun rays, electricity, gasoline, coal, converted to energy by burning, exploding, or magnetic attraction and repulsion.
Programming	The brain a computing, command, memory five sense multi-directive machine with a Rom (Me).	Gears, electronic computers, human hands-on, gauges, tapes-discs, electronic programming and little perception.
Reproduction	The power to reproduce yourself exists.	Lack the power to self-replace.

MACHINES CONTINUED

YOUR BODY WASTE

Feces, urine, perspiration, gases, heat, sloughing off of cells, automatic recycling of bodies through consumption by living nano-sized creatures.

HUMAN DESIGNS

Water, vapor, gases, heat, ashes, corrosion, chemical byproducts. Remains slowly disintegrate by chemical actions of nature.

ME

A special function of an area of your brain.

None

POSSIBLE FUTURE DEVELOPMENT

Increased mental capacity to analyze, organize, and innovate.

Self-consciousness me.

Conclusion: Systems are the building blocks of machines. You are unquestionably a machine.

SEX AND PLEASURE

The design of the human structure includes a number of predilections.

1. Sex - An assurance that the male and female half sets of DNA will have frequent opportunities to unite and initiate pregnancy. The pleasure of the act in the process guarantees the protraction of the species.

2. Hunger - The inauguration of stomach cramps when the stomach empties is replaced by feelings of pleasure when feeding refills the stomach.

3. You possess a hunger for acceptance, praise, respect, and the envy of your peers. This motivates much of the behavior you will perform on life's journey. A sincere compliment to you engenders voluminous pleasure.

4. Raising children elicits a flow of love. Children can bring great pleasure and can generate heartbreaks.

5. There are many other sources of pleasure.

DISEASE AND DECAY

Your body is programmed to deteriorate, which opens the pathways to further debilitation. Live long enough and your life will become pill dependent. You are a natural residence for the world of bacteria, viruses, and fungi. As you age, your circulatory system can clog up; your digestive system can break down; your renal system could build stones, become infected, blocked, and will leak. Your body cells are on the fence of uncontrolled growth. Your perception's senses will lose their efficacy. Your sense of balance will deteriorate. Your bones will grow brittle. Your teeth can rot. Your hair and teeth can fall out. Your muscles will weaken. You can shrink in size. You will have served your purpose on Earth.

But it is not that bad; we are living longer, much longer, more productive lives. Medical researchers have created many crutches. They replace hips, hearts, knees, kidneys, etc. They ream or bypass clogged arteries. They implant electronics to control the actions or inactions of reticent hearts. They monitor and medicate diabetes. They implant teeth and hair, excise appendices, gall bladders, breasts, lungs, testicles, ovaries, intestines, brain and other tumors, uteruses, prostate glands, lungs, etc.

Physicians medicate chemical imbalances, bacterial invasions, excess blood pressure and cholesterol, thick or thin blood, and so forth.

Human machines are supported by a constant flow of new knowledge. A perfect example of the attention that is being bestowed on us. Knowledge, we would not have but for the gifts that are being accorded to us. A good life is achievable.

SPONTANEOUS KNOWLEDGE

We are not alone. We are being tutored by covert mentors. Many spontaneous advances we make are being fed to us through mental flashes. (The study of this phenomenon could make an excellent doctoral dissertation.)

Every human is endowed with specialized talents. These talents are pre-developed mental pathways. Call them natural gifts, special abilities, or aptitudes. What are your superior capabilities? You have some.

New ideas are popularly thought to originate in the brain through the assimilation of knowledge. Our brain, besides being a reasoning, operating, and storage machine is also a reception instrument.

Recall "Eureka, I Have Found It," "What has God wrought," etc.; knowledge is being fed to us as we search for it. Results are proportional to effort.

How many great advances in knowledge were a flash of inspiration or an accidental result? Remember penicillin or the brain flash of Philo T. Farnsworth while operating a mowing machine; the flash that created television.

It is happening all over the world: an accidental result in an experiment or a sudden inspiration solving a seemingly hopeless problem.

A TURN IN THE ROAD

People-kind using the knowledge they have so far accumulated, have put their inventive efforts into designing new mechanical or electronic machines.

Now a new perspective is coming into their views. – Nano technology – we are starting to explore the nano-world. This will open entirely new sciences to us. We will learn how to clone human organs. We will use them to replace failing organs. We are already using donated organs.

If we can correctly connect the new cloned organs together, we should be able to clone a human being. What do you think will be the result of such experiments?

Will the end result be a semi-human, a robot with perhaps a cloned human brain and a mechanical body? If we can conceive of it, then it will be tried.

ROBOTS

The trickle has grown into a stream which will expand into a flood, using computerized robots to design systems that improve human functioning.

A time will come when they not only will assist humans, but they will service their own needs, e.g., robot repairs, manufacturing their own kind. Ultimately, they will have the ability of deciding the wisdom of tasks assigned to them. Robots have no emotions. They will be capable of judging human foibles.

We face an interesting future situation. The competition of two machine systems: The electronic mechanical robot machine versus the human machine. Each will have its own strengths and weaknesses. Will they team together or will they contest for dominance?

IS IT POSSIBLE?

Is it not possible that equipment exists on Earth directing each stage of development of living creatures, or are they disguised edifices, housing knowledge that would be available to an advanced civilization when mature enough to take on an assignment?

There are the mysterious monoliths. Are they more than isolated rock structures, uncovered by flowing water or raised up by earthquakes? Are they more than that, perhaps navigational beacons, warehouses, command posts, operations centers, communication centers, guard posts, well camouflaged with rock wrappings?

Our inability to detect existences that fail to record on the plane of our perceptions should not blind us to the fact that they could exist.

THE STROHS

There are multiple planes of existence, particles that can be bigger and bigger yet, or smaller and smaller yet. At each stage, there are different rules and controls of physics.

Each stage is an association between elements under the rules of existence of that state.

Submicroscopic nano particles form the operating functions of our genes. Particles such as our cells are the building blocks of the living structures of our living universe. Communities of universes form the super cosmos.

Is there a limit to the expansion? Are there strohs smaller than the one below ours, and are there strohs made of a consolidation of upper strohs?

At this time, we have no answers. We can only speculate.

Each stroh has its own environment each stroh is unity unto itself. It can intrude on other strohs, but only by operation of its own unique principles. It is those unique principles that allow the machinery of genes to operate in the realm of our stroh.

Genes are packaged systems of nano apparatuses that direct the construction and operation of giant living beings. They are the architects of all life on Earth both animal and vegetable.

As with any machine, gene defects can cause malfunctions in the beings it constructs. Our present knowledge is only enough to allow us to replace defective genes with healthy genes. We lack the ability of repairing the defect in the gene. The particles of its machinery are so small that we so far have no inkling of how to enter that low a level of a stroh to make repairs.

THE LEVELS OF EXISTENCE

We reside in a level (or stroh) of planets, stars and other stellar bodies, all having influences on each other. We consider ourselves the middle stroh.

There is an upper stroh so vast that our level is but a speck in it. There is a lower stroh that greatly influences our lives. It is the environment of the sub-particles of chemistry. It determines our cells, our structure, our health, our being, and even our thinking.

It forms the working structure of our genes. How small are the particles that turn a gene into an operating structure? A gene is a machine. Its inner working parts are constructed from smaller particles.

Religiously, we think of a Master in heaven above. We need to be aware of the universality of omnipotence. There is masterful organization in the nano-worlds.

To gaze at hypothetical heaven, we look up. We also need to look down. It is the nano-world that creates and operates the machinery of our existence. Consider the possibility of conjectural heaven being in a lower stroh.

OUR STROH

The cell is the building block of our stroh in a system that will build and operate biological machines. It will also destroy and consume foreign biological matter. Cells operate, as programmed, in the various life processes. A strength is the flexibility of the programming. We are working to discover the secrets of the cells' innermost operations. We will succeed.

Each time a particle is reduced dramatically in size, it enters a new plane of properties. Magnetism, gravity, heat, and radiation are properties of a different stage.

Mass results when particles have a strong affinity for each other. Energy is the opposite. It is the end result when there is rejection between particles. Mass and energy are of the same existence, but at opposite poles, as are plus and minus in mathematics, positive and negative in magnetism, gravity, etc.

THE ETERNAL UNIVERSES

Look up to the heavens to find glory. It is there. Now study what we know about the nano-worlds: Look down there too, we find glory.

There is tremendous organization and activity in the nano-strohs, uncountable particle existences that operate on laws of physics running with and counter to the laws of physics of our own existence. There is communication and organization throughout the strohs.

How do power cells actually work? How do microbes develop immunity to antibiotics? What is really going on in the process of photosynthesis? What are the details of the power of sunlight in things such as fading colors or heating its contacts, stimulating growth of vegetation, gravity, magnetism, etc.?

The puzzles are endless. The answers are in the nano and sub nano existences. Needed are extremely inquisitive minds that have the necessary focus to rationalize and the tools to explore the nether worlds.

Answers will come. And when they do, humanity would be able to generate atomic power from water, to mine the ocean bottoms, to produce unlimited food from cell farming, to roam the galaxies, to live longer more youthful lives, and to free humankind from debilitating diseases.

WE DON'T KNOW, BUT WE WILL

Start with the junction of a human sperm and egg. At that instant, there is a switching-on action that initiates a series of developmental processes.

Cell division occurs at a compounding rate. At predetermined stages, cell specializations switch to different types of cells in changed configurations. Rolls of cells start folding into various shapes and inversions, each in the proper proportion to construct a bone skeleton, circulatory piping, a blood-pumping heart. As the cells work, there are created elementary organs, a digestive system, a nervous system, senses, emotions, a reproductive system, muscles, biological clock, etc.

In all of this seemingly organized confusion, there is planning, direction, and design. The genes are following a detailed program of what to do next, and doing it.

The operation is nano and sub nano, with a flow of commands stop, start, change, join, separate, duplicate, so many times, extend, retract, slow down, speed up, enough; each instruction must be given for every cell of tissue.

We don't understand the language of the system of commands, but the time will come when we will.

OUT OF THIS WORLD

When we learn the techniques of growing cells to generate organs, we will have the keys to grow cell masses for other purposes.

Food-Manna from heaven would return to Earth with the flavor of our favorite delicacies, designed to supply all of our nourishment needs, bereft of unhealthy elements such as saturated fats, cholesterol, trans fat, with low or no salt, etc.

By programmed cell development, we would have the ability to grow other needs such as clothing, housing, furniture, roads, buildings, etc.

As living objects, there would be the problems of subsistence, disease control, waste disposal, chemical balances, energy replacement, growth, etc.

When the final shape is reached, the growth process would stop and the object made comatose or more likely euthanized.

There would be need for personnel trained to administer to the ills of biological property. It would be possible, but would it be practical? For most situations, no; for special situations — yes.

CLONING

Primitive procedures of cloning have been published. Anything that is public knowledge will be used. There will be benefits at a price.

Organ cloning will become routine. Exact duplicates of existing organs,but new, youthful and robust. The spare-parts human will become a standard.

These times are the days of exterior body reconstruction. The next step in progress is becoming the days of interior body reconstruction. A great revolution in the medical field is occurring.

TRUE SPACE

True space is not a total vacuum; it is a vast ocean of sub nano-particles. This spectrum operates at a much lower level but much higher volume than our stroh.

The time will come when we will also have the knowledge to utilize the attributes of this stroh to our benefit. We already use it to communicate.

RANDOM THOUGHTS WHY?

In recorded history, there have been numerous epidemics that have decimated major areas of humanity, but rarely totally. Why the limitation?

In the battle between humans and microscopic adversaries, there are times when we have had them in a position of extinction. They mutate, become dormant or develop new hosts. Is smallpox truly totally exterminated?

New diseases are always in the process of germinating. Some may be new, others have been in residence for long periods, non-threatening, then suddenly becoming aggressive. Why?

In every generation, there are despots. Why? Is change itself a system?

Periods of drought come and go. How? Why?

Periods of economic activity grow and decline. How? Why? Is it only human psychology?

Periods of new knowledge flood and ebb. Why?

Nations become world powers, dominate, and then slip back to obscurity — everything is for a short time. Why?

The destruction of the library in ancient Alexandria was a calamity. What knowledge was lost from its vast collection of manuscripts?

Time travel -can it be done? How dangerous is it?

What is the risk of being lost in a wilderness of uncharted time? What effect would time travel have on history? On aging? Are there time barriers?

Was the end of the dinosaur era caused by time or space travel into our sphere? The dinosaurs were a dead end. A new start was needed and was generated. The demise of the dinosaur era was not an accidental phenomena; it was a needed correction.

WHY ARE WE HERE?

Life forms prevail through struggle and anguish to perpetuate their kind.

Humans are endowed with emotional controls and utilize strategies of ego, pride, jealousy, hate, envy, self-righteousness, bravado, contempt, cunning, arrogance, worry, fear, sorrow, revenge, etc.

Every human individual carries a burden of [1] "if only," stress, worry, fear, and regret. The load of stress we carry is constantly being burnished. Stress is so much a factor of human life that it is obviously fundamental to it.

Does the process of stress produce something useful to other existences or is it a form of punishment? Stress, the byproduct of emotion, is debilitating. It is painful.

If we were oysters, an irritant would result in a pearl. With humankind, what could be the valuable bi-product we produce with stress?

Ultimately, we graduate. We are removed from the stress-producing arena, a purpose has been served. We fade into naught.

Could it be we are like cattle, a source of nourishment?

The life stream flows in every generation, recycling matter that was the body substance of previous generations.

---

[1] "IF ONLY" – Life would be a paradise – "IF ONLY" my health was better – "IF ONLY" my spouse was more understanding – "IF ONLY" I was appreciated – "IF ONLY" I had the money – "IF ONLY" I was more attractive – "IF ONLY" I was smarter and so forth.

Is there a soul? Where did it come from? Where does it go? It is not of this world. It could come from the nano strohs or the upper strohs of existence.

The probability prevails that a soul does not exist as an operative unity after death.

Consider human-made machines. Turn on the power and they function as designed. Turn off the power and the machine is a collection of parts (individually useless).

The soul of a human-made machine is the originating idea of its creator. That can also apply to the human being. The soul is the idea of its creator. The soul can be an internal apparatus we call "Me."

HARD TIME - EASY TIME

The question is time-worn what happens to you after you die? For sure, your body decomposes back to the basic chemicals from whence it came. But your soul, where does it go? The spark of life your spirit "Me." Doesn't it move on to a different habitat? No!

Omnipresent in life is stress. There is a partnership of the two. One doesn't occur without the other. Why remains unanswered, but it is universal.

When you die, you are totally free from stress. It can be debated that life is a living hell. Not always true, since there are moments of satisfaction, achievement, and pride. But it is also true that life is heavy with struggle. No matter what your status is in the pecking order, you will still be wearing a pack of "if onlys." Every day has its load of problems to solve.

No individual from the human ranks is exempt from pain, worry, and unhappiness. Also, there is no exemption from death. Death gives you total release from stress. You graduate.

There is no heaven, hell or life hereafter. Your so-called soul returns to what it was, an idea.

ME

"Me" is a function of your brain. When your brain dies, "Me" also dies. "Me" is the nurse and guardian of your machine-body. "Me" is responsible for seeing that you get adequate nourishment, warmth and cooling, rest, exercise, practical education; that you procreate and take care of your young. "Me" has ego, ambition, and an urge to reproduce. It promotes activity and sociability and whatever talents you possess. A specialized part of your brain serves much as the ROM in a computer. It is the master control "Me" of life. It could possibly be located in the brain's neocortex.

"Me" is strongly influenced by your emotions.

HOMOSEXUALITY

Love that is contrary to the reproductive mode is not learned behavior. It is a natural deviancy that is found among bisexual creatures; a departure that may go back to the origins.

It is not an error. It serves a purpose. As a group, homosexuals have unique counterbalancing properties. For a good part, they are bright, artistic, and social. They are community-minded and very creative.

They definitely add a flavor to the mix and may serve an important purposes of which we are not cognizant.

The deviancy exists in the brain's "Me."

FOR THE COMMON GOOD

It is in our tradition that humankind has the ability to distinguish between right and wrong. This could be defined as having the lever of common sense.

A disputer of common sense is "Me"; "What's in it for me." In many circles, that is considered as having basic common sense. "If I don't, who will?" But true common sense is not only aware of the present, but also considers the future in light of the past.

What techniques could we use to control "Me"?

A. Manipulations of the mind to eliminate "Me." As with most things, this solution would have its positives and its negatives.

B. Changing the morés of "Me." A tremendous undertaking that someday will be considered.

C. Gene manipulation with knowledge not yet attained.

D. Coordination so as to make "us" more important than "Me." To prove that benefits to "Us" will bring benefits to "Me."

THE ABSTRACT IS ROUTINE

There are existences that have tremendous power but are not self-operating. They exist in confined spheres. They require interconnects to function.

Ideas — Ideas have dimensions, good and bad, large and small, short-lived to eternal, ancient to new — expanding or shrinking, repudiated to widely accepted, directional to chaotic, repugnant to enticing, immature to mature, trivial to world-shaking, complex to simple — on and on.

Ideas can be owned, patented, copyrighted, advertised, buried, bought, sold, and forgotten. Ideas have time acceptances. Ideas are most important to all phases of life, e.g., entertainment, advertising, business, government, education, medicine, construction, etc. Ideas are the stimulus of human progress and the road to destruction.

You exist because of an idea in action. Upon your death, your body will return to its basic materials, but the idea of your existence can be eternal. Required is a medium for activation and growth. Ideas require projection. They exist in the medium of thought. They endure through projections, as in writing, printing, photography, sculpture, speech, modeling, recording, the media, schools, libraries, memory, construction, invention, etc. Ideas have tremendous power, but they require promotion to reach a pinnacle.

Other abstract powers exist, one of which is "change." It too requires an interconnect to function. There are very few existences that are not under the influence of "change." In all situations, "change" is paired with time. "Change" is an inherent part of materiality.

What about dissent?

COMMUNICATION

You communicate through your perceptions. You see, you hear, you feel, you smell, and you taste.

These senses are used by most of the living creatures on Earth. Bats use sonar; dogs excel in the power of smell. Various animals have different degrees of perceptive keenness.

Humans are using converters to adopt movements of various elements in our five fields of discernment, such as electrical flow in the telephone, radiation in cellular phones, electricity in light generation, electronic discernment of gases, etc.

The likelihood exists that more advanced societies would be using energy flows directly, e.g., magnetism, gravity, and still-unknown forces. Our dependency on multi-frequency electromagnetic radiation limits our ability to communicate with cosmic areas using other media.

You will greatly increase your chances of communication with other life forms in the cosmos when you learn to utilize their systems of exchanging information.

We are not the sole accumulators of communicable knowledge on this Earth. Other forms of life have their own technologies of communicating information with each other. Instinct is not the only answer to the way things are done.

Birds in migration, lions on a hunt, a school of fish in clear water, ants in their search for food, all communicate.

So it is with other life forms living throughout the universes. The limiting factor in communication is that their environments are so different from yours. You could not exist in their environment, and they cannot in yours. You depend on sound waves through air to communicate. They depend on other exotic media to do the same, radiation, temperature alteration, coloration, aberration, brain waves, and innumerable other controllable variables that are totally foreign to us.

LANGUAGE

Communicate we must. In the beginning, it was probably grunts and body movements, as with the various animals. Then, logically designed vocal rumblings evolved as the human voice box became more competent. Specialized sounds were now possible. Further refinement brought phrases, vocabulary, and language rules. Each geographic area develops its own language and rules.

The variations of language complicate human social intercourse. Obviously, a common language is desirable.

For the moment, geopolitics has elevated English into the world's primary language.

LANGUAGE DEVELOPMENT

New forms of language are evolving. Acronyms have become a very popular method of naming creations of our exploding cyber world. The new names are strings of letters, pronouncing each letter. In time, strings of letters need not be only acronyms, they will be self-standing ideas.

A few letters could represent concepts or phrases. We will be communicating in a different code.

At this time, the idea seems very strange and impractical. It would make great literature obsolete. But that would be only part of the price. We must move on. It is the same as saying we shouldn't adopt automobiles because they would make horses and carriages obsolete.

A change will advance technology and generate new forms of literature. It will create a fresh panorama of song, drama, speech, prayer, poetry, etc. . . .

Everything changes — everything.

> DOD - DDPD - ODO - DDDO - DOD
> DOD - ODOD - DOO - DODO - DOD

THE SLIDE TUNER EFFECT

Transmissions on the communication spectrum can be differentiated by varying the frequencies of electromagnetic wave carriers. Other continuances are also delineated by frequencies. As you change the frequencies, you enter a different plane or different time much as you change stations on radio or television.

It is conceivable that other existences operate on the same outline. Could time be such a variable?

If so, could there be a way to change your frequency to transport you to other existences in other frequencies? Physically, it may be impossible, but everything has its exceptions. Gateways could exist.

This could apply not only to time but to existences operating on different planes but occupying the same location.

MORE QUESTIONS

In the search for information of our origins, a popular method has been to dig. In doing so, we find that the deeper we dig, the further back into history we can go.

Question: Where does the material that piles up over ancient civilizations come from? Obvious candidates are the flow of water, windborne dust and soil, debris, volcanoes, human construction, the spread and rotting of vegetation, earthquakes, storms, and insect migrations. Could meteors over millions and millions of years be adding material to the earth's surface? Is there an effect on the rotation of earth?

THE HUMAN ANIMAL

It took less than five millennia for the human population to reach a mass big enough to endanger its environment.

We two-legged human animals are dangerous. We are carnivorous, militaristic, thoughtless, and self-centered. We are prone to lying, cheating, stealing, conniving, and to being untrustworthy, vain, expletive, power-hungry, manipulative, self-indulgent, lacking integrity, morals, reliability, and are frequently lazy. We squander the hopes of future generations and ignore the lessons learned from our predecessors.

All true and yet, there is still a level of concern and decency in every normal human. The forces of good and evil within us are in perpetual combat. Human beings are a frustrating, puzzling element in the level of intelligence.

Through the space reaching electromagnetic emanations we utilize in Earth communications, we inadvertently publicize our earthly cultures to the cosmos. A critical analyzer of our broadcasts can easily conclude that we humans possess a legion of bad traits and are a plague.

←PAIN. . . . . . . PLEASURE . . .→

Pain and pleasure are complementary notes on the same instrument.

Medical researchers have developed medications to dull pain. For deep, unbearable pain doctors resort to narcotics — helpful but addictive. They put the subject into a dreamlike pleasurable condition. To retain the feeling requires more frequent and heavier dosages.

The addictive demand has grown so large that it is a worldwide scourge. Its churn on money has become immense. Distribution of narcotic substances has grown into a tremendous business, in spite of the fact that unprescribed circulation is illegal in most countries.

Being illegal and very lucrative, distribution falls into criminal hands. The tools of illegality: murder, torture, kidnapping, bribes, violence, extortion, robbery, prostitution, gun running, revolution, etc. are utilized. Huge amounts of money are laundered in international trade. Fighting the scourge has almost become a lost cause.

A solution is still possible. Destroy the addictiveness of the substances; much easier said than done, but possible. Find the counteracting agents that will convert the pleasure of usage to agonizing pain.

As with cancer, what is needed is research, research, and research. Such agents exist. Given enough effort, they will be found. Finding a needle in a haystack is always possible if you remove one straw at a time. Is it worth the effort? With drugs, it is.

When discovered, another problem will arise: How to administer it? If it will create a permanent allergy — wonderful. Likely it will require a buildup. Drug rehabilitation programs are already on line. This will hopefully promise a permanent cure.

The target of the substances is to bring the body's receptors into a violent reaction when a specific addictive drug is admitted.

The "con" would be that an individual so treated could not be administered with addictive-type drugs if in great pain, needing relief.

SLEEP

You normally sleep between past sunset to before sunrise when the paucity of light and an excess of fatigue provide a practical reason for inactivity.

Do all living creatures sleep? Do bacteria, cells, fungi, and viruses require inactive periods? Is sleep a universal need in the operating plan of life or semi-life?

On an average, people are unconscious one-third of their lifetimes. If life expectancy is eighty years, twenty-six years of twenty-four-hour days are spent unconscious and unproductive.

A time is coming when humankind will have all the secrets of how the brain receives the messages of new knowledge, stores it, and recalls it.

Technicians will be able to artificially stimulate the brain's activity. They will have the ability to go directly to the nerve ways of the brain, deposit knowledge into its memory banks, and recall knowledge that is stored therein.

The process can be done effectively during sleep. That reduces some of the unproductively of sleep. Dreams prove that there can be brain activity during this period.

To access the knowledge therein without resistance would be possible — a wonderful tool in law enforcement, a stumbling block in espionage.

THE BRAIN

The brain is a glorious machine; every living creature has an organ to direct function. A brain is an intricate maze of operating nano-particles using complex physical, electrical, and chemical laws — most of which are not yet understood.

When they are, we will have the ability to take giant steps in improving our physical and mental foundation. Machines will be used to send signals to our memories in our sleep, greatly accelerating the learning process. We will have the ability to achieve an advanced professional education in weeks. We will bypass learning disabilities. The hiding of experiences would be impossible unless memory was totally erased. Jury trials would be antiquated.

Truth would be readily available, extracted from the brain; we would learn how physical properties are changed into metaphysical ones. For example, how sugar is changed into theories.

As we clone body parts, we would have the ability to clone brains. Does that not mean we would have attained immortality? Never! There will be a loss of function at each cloning, until complete madness would evolve.

The ability to plant information externally into a brain could create a tremendous dilemma for scientists. What would be the results and dangers of using the technology for manipulating the brains of other life forms?

EXTERNAL MANIPULATION OF THE BRAIN

Once we have the ability to insert and retrieve knowledge from the brain, consider the possibilities:

A. Fast education

B. Rapid decisions

C. Controlled behavior

D. Extraction of secrets from the brains of antisocials, criminals, terrorists, and from good citizens, scientists, business executives, government officials, etc.

E. New techniques to repair mental illness

F. Robotic creations

G. Planned divisions of population

H. Brain overload

I. Controlled life habits

J. An autocratic society

Everything has a price.

THE EMOTIONS

Massive research is needed in the nano operations of emotional behavior. Emotions involve electrochemical activity, plus as-yet-unknown technologies.

We have had some success in the study of chemical compounds that have a dampening effect on emotional activity. A few of the discoveries are already in wide distribution. We are totally ignorant of the subatomic operation of these substances on emotion and the cause of side effects.

Since life forms have a common base of design, it is logical that other species also have emotions and personalities.

Emotions, the control valves of human life machines, can be activated both internally and externally. They can be manipulated by charlatans to create violent action murders, riots, lynching, terrorism, cults, cruelty, mass destruction, and population cleansing. It is relatively simple to negate common sense and stimulate fury. Human behavior is programmable.

There are two-sided emotions such as pride, anger, and fear that can be good and bad. And there are good emotions that can also be aroused against injustice, cruelty, greed, and senseless actions, such as pity, guilt, conscience, compassion, and respect.

EMOTIONS AWRY

A big undoing of the human animal is unchecked emotions. Emotions too frequently dominate our relationships. They poison the atmosphere. They initiate precipitous, regretful actions.

As newborns, we are totally innocent and helpless. We learn from our associations. We learn a religion, study habits, eating habits, to love, to hate, habits from the culture surrounding us. Basically, every infant starts as the same raw material. We are shaped by life's exposures,which means we mimic our dominators, our caretakers, and our contemporaries.

Fortunately, an antidote exists: common sense, based on pragmatism. There is some in every human being, but the proportions are inconsistent.

Supposedly, the longer you live, the wiser you get. But that theorem is highly variable, even to the extent of extreme reversal of effect.

The demographics of birth greatly affect our existence on Earth. Common sense can negate the differences, but must be applied and maintained. Economics is a partner in any solution.

PARTIAL LIST OF EMOTIONS

A	B	C
Aggression		Courage
Anger		Confidence
Apathy		Compassion
Affection		Cowardice
Anxiety		Conscience
Annoyance		Contempt

D	E	F
Despondence	Envy	Fear
Delight	Egotism	Frustration
Depression	Ecstasy	
Disappointment	Elation	
Disgust	Exultation	
Distress		
Despair		

G	H	I
Grief	Hope	Insecurity
Gladness	Happiness	Inadequacy
Guilt	Hate	Irritation
Gratitude	Horror	Integrity

J	K	L
Jealousy		Love
Joy		Loneliness

M	N	O
		Obsession

P	Q	R
Pity		Repulsion
Pride		Rage
Pleasure		Regret
		Respect
		Remorse
		Repentance
		Responsibility

S	T	U
Sorrow	Timidity	Unhappiness
Scorn		Understanding
Sadness		Unrepentance
Shock		
V	W	X
Y	Z	

Many of the above are actually degrees of the same emotions. Granted, there are omissions. Space is available to upgrade or correct the list. If you have the itch, please amend it.

WATER

Water is everywhere, but frequently not available when, where, or how it is needed. Earth is generously supplied with water, but we are facing a serious shortage of potable water, our own fault.

The main sources of drinkable water are precipitation, springs, lakes, rivers, wells, melting ice, and small amounts from expensive condensation and desalination systems. The shortfall is growing due to rising population, changes to precipitation patterns, pollution, and waste.

We cannot economically transport pure water in large quantities long distances from areas of surplus to areas of shortage. The idea of aqueducts has been utilized for millennia. It has its limitations. We can recycle more efficiently, and we can capture rainfall better than we are now doing.

An economical method of converting sea water or brackish water into potable water has so far escaped our best efforts.

Nature does it 24/7 through massive evaporation. Can mankind show the organizational aptitude to create so large a project? Perhaps under extreme pressure and at that as a U.W. project.

Liquids have a proclivity to migrate to the surrounding air. Interesting is the fact that the rate of evaporation varies by diverse liquids.

Is the difference in evaporation rate caused by the size of the molecule or are other factors involved? The optimum is to use the day's natural temperature without aids such as heat.

There are techniques to purify water by the generous use of power. When we can inexpensively convert water into power, we will also be able to economically purify water.

WATER

We can not cheaply filter the impurities out of the sea water, but various marine creatures live in and ingest salty sea water without their flesh becoming salty.

What process does nature use to filter out the salt and other chemicals? The time will come when we will be able to adopt more of nature's techniques.

Our needs on Earth are available in adequate supply. Water is an ideal source of power. There are methods other than steam, gravity, and hydroelectric dams to create huge outputs of water power. They are scheduled for development.

$H2O$ is available throughout the universes, making it a logical fuel for space travel. On occasions, it will be necessary to tanker water to various space locations. On other occasions, water will be available as a byproduct of numerous procedures.

As our knowledge of the sub-strohs grows, we will ultimately learn how to economically separate compounds into their basic elements. We will be able to inexpensively process $H2O$ into $H2$ and O.

It will be possible to transmit these gases over special conduits, long distances, where they will be reconstituted into pure water.

At this time, it is a dream in the future, routine.

A TIME WILL COME

A time will come when the human race will achieve the knowledge of how to alter the strength and direction of the binding ties that create mass.

Much as temperature determines the hardness of certain types of matter, there are other forces that also perform the same function.

High temperatures convert water to gaseous steam, and low temperatures reduce the liquidity of water to rock-hard ice.

It will be possible to use these new powers to convert water to controlled degrees of hardness without relying on temperature. The resultant material will be manipulatable. We will be able to use the amended substance, much as we now use plastics.

By passing discarded products made of this material through special home-based machines, we will have the ability to return them back into liquid matter. There will be drainage systems to carry the affluent to specialized factories that will recycle it. This material will not burn and will resist melting. It can be very thin and flexible – very thin and rigid.

Garbage collection and garbage dumps will be obsolete. Humans will have stronger control over pollution and waste. Wood will be a basic material of the past. Forests and the wild life therein will flourish.

THOUGHTS OF MARS

Will Mars be the site of humankind's first space colony? In these early years of proposed space travel, Mars is being given concentrated attention.

We reside on a planet stocked with the resources to maintain human civilization. Inhabiting a space body, earthlings require the availability of the same resources that are available on their natural abode. The problem is that we haven't found a hospitable planet, not even Mars. Our poles, which offer training in living in a hostile atmosphere, already possess a breathable atmosphere.

Mars appears to have gone through a resource change in its history. Surveillance has indicated that the surface of the planet may have been inundated with water, now gone except for ice accumulation at the poles.

Speculation: If true, Mars's population (if there was one) moved underground and took the water with them, or a major portion of Mars's water was moved off the planet, some to Earth, the balance elsewhere.

As has been noted, water has tremendous power potential. It is the fuel of our future. The fact that we do not have the knowledge to use it atomically does not mean that other space civilizations are not doing so.

Space engines of the future will create gravity. Gravity has the properties of both attraction and repulsion. Proper use of those abilities at the same time will develop great speed in space and provide braking ability and internal gravity for the passengers' comfort.

OVERPOPULATION

In the near future, numerous older diseases will be conquered. Food production will be exponentially increased. Wars will be criminal acts. Life expectancy will lengthen. Further, populations will explode.

Decisions will have to be made. Religions will have to be rethought. Is it God's intention to have human beings drown themselves in a flood of themselves? We are created with common sense. Is it a sin to use God's gift?

A few ideas on population control:

A. Should reproduction be forcibly controlled by government? Science will eventually be able to block fertility by a single pill, male and female.

B. Should lifespans be controlled through painless euthanasia? Death will become recognized for what it is — a graduation, a natural stage of life.

C. Should there be forceful colonization of the cosmos to drain off excess population?

D. Will the population be divided into classes — thinkers and workers?

E. Life could become so stress-free that many couples would set a limit of no children. It may become a function of the government to produce and raise children.

Raising children adds greatly to stress. "Yes, when they are small, they are small problems and when they get big, they become big problems." As the government social programs improve, children will be unnecessary to provide for old age, their main advantage in many societies.

There is no forgetting that children are our future. A basic goal of life is continuation. Children add spice and pleasure to living, as well as stress.

It is conceivable that someday, our population will so explode that Earth would increasingly be stripped of vegetation to recycle the atmosphere, resulting in a shift of balance between oxygen generation and carbon dioxide generation. Humans would be in danger of poisoning themselves.

HUMAN CAPITAL

Healthy human bodies are capital. The larger the population available, the larger is the ability to affect standards. The results are proportionate to the wisdom of utilization.

Dealing with humans means that the element of self-will is always present. Forceful use always generates resistance and depreciates the value of the capital. Keeping the population happy and interested in projects expands the value of human capital.

This has been known by intelligent leadership from time immemorial. One problem has always been the shortness of life. Leadership is constantly changing. New leadership rarely has the goals and inclinations of the old. Experiences are always different; therefore, outlook will be different.

As with any problem, compromises are required. We find it necessary to plan with averages.

OUR DESTINY

Homo sapiens are complicated machines, but in the final analysis, chemo/mechanical/electrical machines. We have the ability to control ourselves, but we are also very controllable remotely, as previously outlined.

Why are we here? There is no hint. We do serve a purpose. If we survive, the human race will travel to other space localities. We will colonize them. Ultimately, we will interact with other intelligences. We will multiply and create vast civilizations.

"Nothing is forever - as it had been, it need not be - and it will not be."

We are on assignment.

EUTHANASIA - GRADUATION

In our time slot of the road of existence, the popular view on euthanasia is that it is criminal murder. It invades the provenance of divinity. There is merit to that view, but the view also supports extreme hypocrisy. Abortions and euthanasia are criminal murder but military slaughter is not. Perpetrators of the former are vilified but of the latter are honored, be-medaled, and adulated for their brave patriotism. Success in war has been measured by body counts. Accessory killings are forgiven as risks of the game.

Death in the case of abortion and euthanasia is performed as a highly individualized procedure. War deaths are programmed on a playing field of mass butchering.

Needed for the peace of society is world legislation to try to convert abortions into adoptions without criminalizing them. To have euthanasia approved by quick-acting, sympathetic professional boards with rights of swift appeal, consideration of patients' viewpoint if they are responsible enough at the time or had written authorization in previous lucid years, or presently meet certain standards, then euthanasia should be allowed.

Medical science is extending the good quality of life, but a time comes when unbearable pain or collapse of function reduces life to a torturous or vegetative existence, an agony to loved ones and caretakers, and of no value to the subject. There is need of a legal release mechanism to accomplish the inevitable.

Death is the last obligation of life. It is a graduation from the burdens of living. After death, the suffering is transferred to the mourners. They have lost a supporter who had helped mitigate the stress in the mourners' lives. Time brings adjustment.

We are well aware there will be among the survivors those who will be inwardly happy about the demise of persons with whom they had a relationship, a human trait.

Abortions must still be available to those women who have deep feelings to want them. Childbearing should never be instituted as a punishment for being human.

RELIGION

Is it only the human animal who feels lost on Earth, feels inadequate, forlorn and helpless, battered by fate?

Going back to the beginning of evidential history, we find our early ancestors prayed to idols made of baked clay, stone, or wood (later metal) which they felt were superior beings, deities who could control and improve the life of the worshipers.

In various populated areas of the world, myths evolved concerning the comings and goings of the deities. These omnipotent supposedly had humanlike qualities. They lived in communities and had emotions such as love, tempers, and jealousies.

Three and a half millennia ago, the patriarch of a small Semitic family became the originator of a new concept, the existence of only a single all-powerful "Almighty." This "all powerful" also displayed human emotions.

With the advent of Christianity, the Hebrews' deity became a Father, and with the writings of Mohammed, a third religion took root over much of the Earth, based on the same single Almighty God of the Hebrews, flavored with respect for the early tales of the Old Testament, the New Testament, and the teachings of Mohammed the prophet.

This led to a sad state of affairs. The three major religions recognize the same single original Almighty Deity, yet the adherents have a history of aversion to each other.

All three religions condemn the act of murder. Two of them have histories of violently killing non-observers. When will common sense finally rule?

For the most part, people assume the religion of their birth families. Most people of the world, who look to religion as a comfort, accept the existence of a single God. In the case of Christianity, it is the trinity as a single godhead.

Why can't we live and let live? The majority follow the lines of a religion by accident of birth. They are indoctrinated in childhood. This doesn't make them superior or inferior.

A PRIORITY

There is a requirement for a system that early in life recognizes a child's strong points. A plan must be devised to usher each child in the direction of his or her strengths – everybody gains.

This will do much to lead the individual to a lifetime of motivation and feeling of self-worth. The resulting pride, recognition, and potential prosperity will become the crown of a useful life. How many present social problems could be avoided?

It is common knowledge that success is achievable through motivation. If we feel we are good at it, we enjoy doing it and are motivated to apply ourselves with maximum effort.

HUMAN WORTH

People have reached a position in development where we can make giant steps forward or regress back to the caves.

We have the weapons of mass destruction. We maintain the ego-feeding philosophies of our existence — we are the greatest — our culture is the advanced correct one — our religion is the only true one — our language is superior — our lifestyle is a leader for the world. We are the trendsetters for the world in all important things. The illusions go on and on throughout the nations of the world.

These mindsets are a part of our problems. It is time to mature. It is time to recognize that all humans are the same. The only difference is the cultures where we grew up. If by fate we grew up elsewhere, our lifestyle would be as found therein. Accept the truth.

Humankind must start thinking globally. Our technology has moved us into a global theater. Every person has the same worth as every other person, regardless of color, religion, gender, affluence, talent, and fortune (good or bad). Equality must be universal.

We will have only a limited control over a person's drive, but worldwide opportunity can be equalized.

THE CASINO OF LIFE

Being born on earth as a human being, involves you in more gambling than can be found in any casino on the planet. Your life here is strictly predicated by random happenings. Human living is fate-controlled.

It starts with the location of your birth – a hospital, at home, a tent, a ditch. What is your sex? What is your race? What is the financial situation of your family? Is your religion a majority or minority in your birthplace? Are you born in a tribal culture, majority, or minority? Is there any education available? Is there adequate food, adequate medical care, adequate shelter or clothing? Is the country of your birth developed or third world? Is the government progressive or regressive? Is the country's economy growing or stagnant — starvation level or opportunistic? What is the human life expectancy in the country of your residence? What fortuitous happenings occur in your life? How healthy are your birth genes? What are your talents?

A majority of babies adapt to their environs. They are patriotic to their homelands. They assume the prejudices of their surroundings. They embrace the local culture, language, dress code, and religious values. For the most part, the lifestyles of their birthplace becomes the baggage they carry through life. We all carry our own baggage.

THE GAMBLE OF LIFE

Lifestyle is dependent on a toss of the dice. When born, all infants are equal. They eat, cry, laugh, sleep, fuss, urinate and defecate at will, instinctively. They learn to walk and talk, and need to be toilet trained.

From then on, their environment takes over.

Children should be entitled to an equal playing field at that stage. Education helps in many places. It is considered a birthright. Motivation is another thing.

We need to take it to the next level. We need to have our talents assessed and our best should also be promoted by public funds, the same as is budgeted for public education.

Society would be the gainer - a win-win situation. The hold back "There is no money." If it were a life-or-death situation, money would appear. The problem is a global one. "I am my brother's keeper." Think U.W.

CIVILIZATIONS, PAST, PRESENT, AND FUTURE

Certain points in history stand out. Civilizations had spurts of creativity in various enclaves and at specific time periods. What brought on these patches of inspiration, stimulated technical advancement, and produced innovative thinking?

Evaluate the social and economic status of the time. There was prosperity, stable government, leisure time, minimal unrest, and surplus capital, a condition that only arrives in random fashion.

We have recently again entered the upside of such a cycle. New inventiveness and changes are once again in our midst. We are holding worldwide meetings to further advance common sense; we are trying.

There are strong feelings among our populace that we should help our neighbors. Let us be mindful that ours is not the only way to do things.

Let us live and let live. Let us learn from each other. Unfortunately, we must always remain vigilant. Evil is alive and well at all times and in all places.

AND IT SHALL COME TO PASS

1. The basics of life: food - shelter - clothing - heat - education and career direction will be produced with great efficiency.

2. The common government will be an upgraded democracy with capitalist underpinnings. These standards have proven to be the most productive.

3. Manufacturing will be totally automatic, machine produced, using computers, robots, force fields, etc. Health programs, paid layoffs, pensions, or wage disputes will no longer appear in the production process. Production costs of all the former countries will be basically equal.

4. Medical care will largely be done by machines. Defective body parts will be replaced by custom-designed clones.

5. There will be pressure to treat human reproduction as a machine function – emphasizing superior genes, induced conception, incubation of the fetus till birth proportions, and governmental child raising.

6. The primary labor of humans would be in planning, R & D, government, pioneering, culture, supervision, education, entertainment, care giving, law enforcement, sports, transportation, service, construction, maintenance, business, warehousing, food production and preparation, health, legal, tax, and financial endeavors.

7. Stress will be greatly reduced.

8. Life expectancy will be vastly lengthened.

9. New generations being fresh dynamic forces will receive great attention. Seniors will be indulged until a reason for living ceases to exist.

10. Mental treatment centers will replace prisons.

11. Global warming will receive the attention needed.

12. The world's dependence on oil will disappear.

13. Wars will become a footnote of our primitive era.

14. The human, being human, will continue as a problem in every situation. Discontents will remain among us no matter what improvements develop.

WE ARE OBLIGATED

Strong reproductive impulse has made birth rates high and the value of life low. Undisturbed, humankind can quickly outgrow their food supply.

Fortunately, science has increased food production proportionately in developed countries. In undeveloped countries, there is still the travail of famine.

When misfortune overtakes any section of humanity, it becomes the moral responsibility of those more fortunate anywhere on Earth to come to their aid. Misfortune lurks in every nook. Nobody has it made. Everybody living is scheduled for disaster.

Today it is your turn to suffer. Tomorrow it will be my turn. A person only for himself is an anomaly who is doomed to ultimate despair.

LET US HONOR

This is a good time and place for us to pay homage to our own ancestors who suffered greatly to bring us to this stage in human history. We must use our inherited responsibilities to leave this a better world than the one we were born onto. In too short a time we will be joining them.

We have already been blessed. The level of human education is the highest it has ever been. Worldwide, standards of living have grown, but you can make things much better. If not you- who?

COMMON SENSE

You live in a world immersed in hate, murder, jealousy, disease, addiction, terror, and economic uncertainty.

You probably consider yourself as a member of an advanced civilization. You look back on our predecessors as primitive.

Yes, we have made progress. In the past, warring nations could slaughter by the tens of thousands. Now with less effort we can do it by the millions. A questionable improvement, but definitely a rise in efficiency.

There is a dire need of human relationship improvement. We know better but we lack the determination to solve major problems. It is common sense that we are not living up to our potential.

There is the United Nations, a futuristic concept, but a disabled one. One hundred ninety-plus nations commune to play politics. The controlling factors of the game are emotion and cunning dealing.

Leadership is well aware of their limitations. Their hands are too often tied. To be able to attack many problems requires the bypassing of the United Nations, as was started by the creation of NATO.

COMMON SENSE II

The mission of the voyage of Starship Earth is to serve as a catalyst in organizing conditions in an assigned spatial region.

In our present stage, we would be poor ambassadors to try to sell a concept that we ourselves have not accepted. We recognize that there is great need for a better way to administer things. But we are constantly being diverted by emotion. We are not yet ready to approach our misunderstandings with common sense.

In every endeavor, there are scoffers trying to hide their own inadequacies with bombast. They are not the progenitors of advanced concepts. They are the roadblocks of progress.

There will be ample opportunities to test this conjecture.

THE TIME HAS COME

Knowledge in the fields of medicine, communications, chemistry, physics, astronomy, nano technology, and computer science is advancing in giant steps.

But the governmental and political disciplines are moribund. Progress is restrained by outpourings of poisonous emotion in political fray.

The time has come to give priority to revising the trend before we find ourselves in a cataclysm.

The flood of technology has us drifting into globalization. Let us set the course. The concept of globalization is not evil. Harmful effects are the work of incompetent management. The administrative body of a global government must be highly qualified at all times.

It will be far less complicated operating a single arena than it has been with almost 200 independent nations. Some day, humankind will look back at our time of life and evaluate this era as a rudimentary age.

ACTION REQUIRED

Crises are increasingly influencing the well-being of the humans who inhabit the Earth. The global reach of technology requires a global solution to these emergencies. The world is divided into more than 200 sovereign countries, making practical conclusions almost impossible at this time.

A sampling of major problems facing us are:

1. Terrorism — An insidious poison difficult to eradicate.

2. Global warming caused by the mismanagement of chemicals and by the burning of fossil fuels.

3. Human, animal, and plant diseases, new or newly resistant to formerly successful defensive measures.

4. Ethnic cleansing — Humans murdering humans, driven by primitive emotions.

5. Poverty due to lack of natural resources, lack of education, lack of capital, and rule by self-indulgent governments.

6. Availability of the raw materials of weapons of mass destruction.

7. Famine, epidemics, drought, floods, earthquakes, out-of-control fires, pest invasions, and other disasters.

8. Economic collapse, hyper-inflation, poor fiscal management, monopolistic control of some of the Earth's resources.

Solutions or amelioration can be made available by a central world government that truly has the interests of its citizens at heart. The need is so great that if we don't destroy ourselves first, a world government will evolve.

SURVIVAL OF THE FITTEST

A foundation of the theory of evolution is that living creatures thrive or perish by their success in adapting to changes in their environment.

The human being, a living animal, is naturally subject to these laws. The human has become dominant because of the development of its ability to originate new tools and to organize happenings.

The ability has its weaknesses. New tools and happenings come with side effects, some capable of destroying the human race. The power to destroy is magnified in the wrong hands.

Unless we act as a totally united group, this effect will prove irresistible to the rogues leading some of our 200 nations and their satellite terrorist groups.

What can we do about it? We can modify our lifestyles to convert 200 nations to a single worldwide country, the United World. The full force of all humans will be applied to control the evils. Survival of the fittest will continue for the human race.

A START

Required would be a select group of some of the world's most open-minded, innovative, wisest people who have lived with all aspects of the world, without pretensions, people who are aware of their prejudices and can control them.

People of integrity with common sense, vision, and the ability to make painful compromises are needed, no prima donnas. Their task would be to establish and staff an institute of world stature.

The objective would be to lay the groundwork through publicizing, promoting, and designing the framework of a planet wide government, U.W. "The United World."

An initial task of the institute would be to educate the people of the planet with the reasons for the need and the benefits of a world government. A joint task would be to organize a plan of steps needed to initiate such a government, and thirdly the constitution and organization of this new government — leaving local control to handle local problems — subject to United World veto.

The institute must be apolitical, non-religious, free of any commercialism and personal influence from any persons or governments. It must try to anticipate and solve contingencies. Auxiliary projects will develop.

It must prepare plans for various levels of governing, health programs, economic controls, and so forth.

Methods need to be devised to substantially raise the living standards of former third world nations. Automatic poverty must be eradicated. Areas of high living standards must retain those standards.

The institute will study the historical events that led to wars, and design assurances that these conditions will not return. Being a one-country world, the former craving for territorial expansion will cease to exist – so will closed borders.

There will always be an undercurrent to consider breaking the world union into enclaves, since the abstract power "dissent" is always present.

THE UNITED WORLD GOVERNMENT (U.W.)

The task assigned to the institute will be grueling and complicated. It will be a forward-working plan to bring political science up to date.

From initiation to installation could take generations. Opposition driven by rabble rousers and arch conservatives will flourish. U.W. advocates will be ridiculed and threatened. The early years of any world change movement initially are difficult.

Every human being is equal. Every human is entitled to honor and respect when they do a conscientious job on their life's chosen work. Their professional rating must not be judged by the unpleasantness of the work they do, but by the standards they set in doing repugnant and boring work which must be done. Ratings and compensation will be directed only by performance.

THE U.W.

Common-sense standards must replace the former measurements of values based on wealth, physical attractiveness, athletic agility, personality, luck, popularity, youth, craftiness, connections, and religion.

The members of the originating committee and the subsequent institute should serve for predetermined terms with pensions. Thereafter, they would be available as consultants with compensation.

The objective is to create a government that will promote human tranquility and satisfaction to maintain a government with a maximum of cooperation and a minimum of friction among its citizens.

Emotions must be shackled and the fresh air of common sense released to become our new environment.

THE BEGINNING

Financing is critical. With the temptation of using money to influence, all financial fundraising must be unqualified donations minimum twenty-five cents to unlimited. Taxation will ultimately be required.

A record must be kept of every donation received, no matter how small or large. Financing must be very strictly monitored, with audited published reports under the control of a limited board with staggered terms.

Moderation will be the standard of all decisions. Nepotism will not be tolerated.

Rotation is required. Previous officeholders must be available for consultation. A channel must always be open for minority concerns. Perfection is impossible, but improvement is attainable.

There are mutual advantages for the institute to have ties with higher institutions of learning, provided the institute is free from all control therefrom. Worldwide institute branches are a must. Frequent exchange is essential. The controlling principle in all findings must be common sense. Trial and error is to be expected. When mistakes occur, they must have quick recognition and have high priority for correction.

There will be no compromises to try to get the cooperation of nations looking for an edge. All functions must be initiated and maintained on equality. This will require courage, but long-term success is impossible otherwise.

ONE WORLD

One world — the United World — an idea ridiculed and supposedly extinct, but not so. The idea has been hibernating in a fetal state. Its time had not yet come. Conditions have changed, with a worldwide conspiracy of radicals using terrorism as their weapon. Even if eventually subjugated, they will leave footprints of the possibility of worldwide blackmail by any misguided possessors of the latest advanced killing technologies. This situation will cause a rapid maturation of the formerly comatose concept of a truly united world.

In many ways, elements of one world have been accepted. Operative are various facets of a one-world society — the Internet, satellite communications, international television, entertainment, jet aircraft, international outsourcing, the World Bank, the International Monetary Fund, cooperative worldwide medical research, the Red Cross, the United Nations, NATO, NAFTA, the Olympics, international businesses, the E.U., the I.A.E.A., W.T.O., international philanthropy, economic and environmental world conferences, worldwide retail chains, multinational conglomerates, on and on, with the list steadily growing.

The united world concept will be feared by many who possess wealth and power or covet them. They fear that conditions will change contrary to their benefit. They will try many schemes to derail U.W. acceptance.

There are others who fear that a super world government would become a monster, a possibility that exists with any government. The problem is not the structure of government, but the leaders of it. (Decayed food will make a disaster of any banquet.) Humans have a naiveté streak. They are easy subjects of manipulation. They are very self-centered.

These are conundrums that need to be handled by the architects of the new unity. It is their problem to resolve. Checks and balances are critical; wise minds must consider many stumbling block problems and find viable solutions; compromise will be a necessary keystone. Responsibility cannot be compromised.

An obvious question will be asked. We have the U.N., why not tweak it to make it more available? It won't work. The U.N. was a stopgap. It was specifically designed to operate in the cold war. It was the best that could be gotten. Its basic structure is unbalanced, unfair.

The need will be for a carefully designed constitution as soon as possible to publicize the advantages of a modern government. It must be of advantage to a worldwide population and be responsible for the welfare of every living human being.

No dictators, no elites, no royalty, no world power ogres, no warlords, no oligarchies, no economic or religious potentates. It must provide for an operating authority free of partisan restraints under the rule of checks and balances.

Throughout human existence on Earth, there have been the poor, struggling to survive, many not succeeding. There are millions today in that position. It is within our power globally to correct that situation.

All life only has a limited time here. We can exist until it is time to go or we can make a mark in the short time we are here. We can leave it a better place than we found it.

We have it within our aptitude to make choices for which future generations will have a reason to honor our memory. The establishment of a U.W. will be one of those choices. Hopefully, it will not take a war, wars, or mass terrorist killings to get a universal concurrence on the advantages of worldwide government.

The advantages are profuse. Only a few are a single currency, open trade worldwide, a common banking system, a single language, open borders, worldwide police system, immediate assistance after any disaster, all embracing medical aid and controls, monies diverted from the former military to higher standards of living, to research, and the elimination of disastrous competition between nations.

WAR AN EVIL

War the seductress — it entices with offers of seemingly guaranteed achievement of goals through the use of irresistible force, but it is a false enticement.

Research history — How long do the results last unless there is total annihilation? Resistance continues to effervesce. If it doesn't, in a generation the former antagonists find it advantageous to utilize each other's resources and good graces. This would have been a good idea in the beginning. They should have skipped the killings.

War is exhausting, wasteful, and unintelligent. Better ways are readily available. Why must emotions run their course before common sense takes hold?

Why must there first be mass killing, a generation of widows, orphans, disabled, famine, unemployment, hatred, destitution, epidemics, and shortened lifespans?

All could be avoided by negotiation, mediation, and unbiased truth.

If all fails, then the dispute should be submitted to a United World Supreme Court of Justice, whose decision would be final — provided in it both sides must gain, both sides must lose. Justice would rule — not law.

THE PLAN

Nations and organizations of the world accumulate huge stocks of weapons to use to kill and destroy in disputes with other human dominions. What they stock for the purpose is soon obsolete or worn out. Constant expenditures are needed.

A beneficial aspect is that many persons are gainfully employed in jobs soldiering, recruiting, training, transporting, repairing, warehousing, housekeeping, manufacturing, designing, medical care, clerical, etc. This stimulates the economy by the injection of massive sums of money into it, largely borrowed with interest due. If there is military action, reconstruction is needed, a further injection into the economy.

Had the same resources been applied to building up the productive base of the country, the living standards would have taken a larger, more permanent rise.

War makes no common sense. It must be banned. There are better ways. New standards for settling disputes must be adopted. War makers must be subject to the most extreme punishment. Ways to settle disputes can be:

1. A mediation process.

2. If unsuccessful, an arbitration process.

3. The result could be appealed to a "U.W." Supreme Court of Justice, separate from a Supreme Court of Law. This court would not rule on the law or the constitution. It would give a decision based on common-sense justice.

4. Their decision must be approved by a board accepting it if it offers adequate loss and gain to both parties. With their approval, the court's findings would be final. Rejection

would assign the case to a different Supreme Court of Justice.

5. If there is still no resolution, it would revert to a supreme arbitration board for a no-appeal decision.

THE TOP JOB

What does it take to merit the top office of a world government? As in everything else, luck is prime. Influential connections are crucial. Dealing in favors is basic, money is essential, "What's in it for me" is most important.

Also paramount is personal appearance, charm, family, campaign management, religion, hobbies, and advanced education. A forceful personality is considered an indication of leadership.

These are the things on which we stake our lives and fortunes when we vote. We frequently get what we deserve.

There has to be a better way of selection and there is. In many human resource departments of major corporations, the management has researched better ways to locate quality candidates to fill their openings. They've developed testing techniques that are helpful. Why not use these new tools in securing the most qualified candidates for top government positions?

If the results are an improvement over the haphazard election practices of the past, then the knowledge gained should be applied to secure the leading talent for positions that so affect the life of each of us.

Security of tests on such a system would require the services of geniuses. Geniuses are available.

OPPOSITION

There will be intense opposition to the one world proposal. Sometimes vocal, sometimes demonstrative, sometimes violent but always subversive with a cacophony of spewing falsehoods.

A major consideration of the institute will be as to how to maintain a defensive posture. Opposing riots will be designed to generate antipathy. The institute's most effective defense will be to flood the world with truth.

The opposition's stock rebuttal will be to malign the institute's proposals as blatant propaganda. An organized, steady barrage of truth will eventually become unassailable and will decimate the opposition.

All major changes in the world's progression seem to necessitate upheaval. It will require supreme effort to overcome inertia.

Many countries of the world are ruled by governments strongly opposed to "democracy" — the governmental foundation of "The United World." Wisdom will be needed to achieve success.

THE LABORATORIES

Count the number of countries that are the precursors of the world to come. They have acted as havens for humans in distress — those humans who have been lucky enough or clever enough to escape the atmospheres of their birthplaces, averting lives of poverty, subjugation, starvation, incarceration, stifling morés, prejudice, hopelessness, and death.

These refuge countries have acted as laboratories, studying and developing methods of integrating diverse populations into a single unit where all parties will act for the common good. Envy, hate, malice, and clannishness must be suppressed. Homogeneous enclaves and states must open their gates. Tribalism must be recognized as archaic.

Paradise will not come to Earth, but a forward movement of human intelligence dictates change. We will finally understand that our actions heighten stress. Stress is a condition we must exist under during our sojourn on Earth. It cannot be eliminated, but it can be reduced.

THE FINEST HOUR

The president of the United States will face a dilemma, being the leader of a powerful government.

The president's political party will firmly control the government. The opposition is only a shadow. The overwhelming number of votes of the president's constituency will guarantee a lion's share of the congressional seats, and at the same time there will be in office only one justice of the Supreme Court who had not been nominated by the present party in power.

A worldwide movement will be actively advocating "one world." That would denigrate all countries to the status of provinces. What will be the president's decision? It will set the course of history for the human race for generations to come.

Will this become her finest hour? Will she dare to make a decision that could lead her compatriots to vilify her as a traitor and a squanderer of the nation's pride of grandeur?

The same will apply to all the leaders of the balance of the world's nations. Can common sense run deep enough? Must people-kind first face extinction?

BEWARES OF THE FUTURE

1. Beware of turning living creatures into robots.

2. Beware of turning elitist groups into world powers.

3. Beware of the easy availability of weapons of mass destruction.

4. Beware of limiting population growth too stringently and the converse of allowing it to explode.

5. Beware of the loss of the work ethic.

6. Beware of the failure of monitoring the trends of human mental health, general health trends, and population opinions.

7. Beware of the growth of militarism under any guise.

8. Beware of the breakdown of the systems of checks and balances in any department of administration.

9. Beware of allowing resentments to fester.

10. Evil comes in many forms, even in the guise of working to overcome evil.

11. Beware of a total dominance of science.

12. Beware of the revival of barbarism.

13. Beware of prolonged artificial alterations of cycles that can change natural balance.

14. Beware of laissez-faire.

15. Beware of a return to sectionalism.

16. Beware of lackadaisical frequency of communication with subdivisions.

17. Beware of monopolies.

18. Beware of indifference.

19. Beware of the return of emotionalism.

20. Beware of the lack of mechanisms to allow the release of emotional pressures.

21. Beware of the paralysis of democratic controls.

22. Beware of boredom, fatigue, and cults.

23. Beware of a sudden change in basic life requirements without counter-adjustments.

24. Beware of chicanery, bluffing, lying, falsifying, bribery, and manipulation.

25. Beware of failure to include the entire human race into a single system.

26. Beware of outside influences plotting the destruction of beneficial systems.

27. Beware of misplaced trust; diligence is critical. Everything, everyone has good and evil. Beware of excessive oppression.

28. Beware of considering this list complete.

A world government is scheduled to occur. It will have many trying times. We are here under stress; nothing can eliminate that, but life on Earth will be more pleasant.

IT WAS THE BEGINNING OF TODAY

A time came when the central government decision makers were unwilling to forgo their inclinations. They decided to cater to their own self-interests. They refused to accept the painful sacrifices needed to defuse a threatening situation.

Their failure to act initiated the contamination of the air, the ground, the water, and the food supply. The greatly advanced civilization on their own spaceship planet ceased to exist.

This possibility had been foreseen. The dominators were only one of the many designs of life forms on board, other life forms survived the slaughter. Their civilizing growth rate slowly accelerated, their size and brain power gradually enlarged, their numbers increased.

The assignment to mediate in space exploration still stood. Another life form would assume the responsibility of performing it.

Only a single galactic colony of this sovereignty remained unscathed. The settlers on it faced a failure of resupply and were aware that their future survival was questionable.

They considered the prospect of leaving a monumental memorial to establish the fact that they had resided on the colony planet. That idea was discarded after they realized that in time the memorial would disintegrate. Instead they adopted an idea that could last an aeon.

All native creatures on the resident planet were locked into mental rigidity. It would be a great advance if the colonists could correct that for even a single specie. This would serve as their memorial and a possible transfer of their assignment.

The colony members created a list of minimum standards and decided which one of the native species most closely approached those standards. They assembled a group of the chosen ones-male and female, anesthetized them, and added to their genome specialized genes that gave the chosen the ability to innovate and to organize-competences that had served their own genre so well.

The chosen would now become the dominators of this colony planet and would determine its future. The modified species of homo sapiens, through introgression, spread over the surface of planet Earth. It was the beginning of today.

Genesis 1:27

"so the Almighty created man in his image,
in the image of himself he created him; male and female
he created them."

Genesis 2:21

"so the Lord set a deep sleep upon the man
And he slept; and he took of his body
And he replaced flesh in its place"

STOP THE CLOCK

The Bulletin of the Atomic Scientists have been publishing a clock with its hands close to midnight. Midnight is the figurative end of the human world, when the world would reach an atomic and a various other threatening events point of no return. The Bulletins Board of Sponsors now includes 18 Noble Laureates.

They started in 1947. The hands have moved back and forth. The closest to disaster was 1984. The hands stood at 3 minutes before midnight. 1991 it was 17 minutes to midnight. For 2007 these great minds have put the hands at 5 minutes to midnight. We are that close to a global cataclysm.

It is not too late, if we can inaugurate one world [The United World] expeditiously—no time lost. We must STOP the clock.

JULIAN H. HYMAN – A BIOGRAPHY

Born August, 1920 Hyman is today an eighty-plus years old senior who has lived an active life in the history of his surroundings. In his eightieth year he under went a triple by-pass. The knowledge of performing this operation was given to human kind only recently. For his age he is in good health.

His childhood was enacted during a grinding world-wide depression. In his family money was tight. but he did not lack for any of life's' essentials. He had three sisters-no brothers..

In first grade he showed a tendency to be left handed. His sisters fearing a freak brother used force to correct the supposedly harmful condition. A second problem appeared-he was behind in his class in learning to read. At that time the condition was considered retardation. Today we call it dyslexia.

Hyman excelled in mathematics with no retardation. Once he got the feel for reading he became a book addict. He would leave the public library needing both hands to carry his resupply. For high school he was assigned to the city's male advanced public academic high school where he flourished. Toward graduation he applied to only one college- The University of Pennsylvania's Wharton School of Commerce. He received early acceptance.

During the last half of his senior college year the country was attacked at Pearl Harbor. The United States was at war. Circumstances allowed him to graduate college. Soon thereafter he enlisted in a program sponsored by the Army Air Force. The Air Force was short of low rank officers with certain skills. It instituted an accelerated cadet training program for recent college graduates.

It started with a basic training regimen at the stripped down former Boca Raton Hotel in Florida. They concentrated the disciplines of the military academies into five months. Cadets were exposed to all the pressures of those schools to test them; if they could prove themselves officer material. If the candidate passed basic he moved up to Yale University for various technical training still as a cadet for additional months.

Hyman remembers the white glove inspections of the cadet's quarters in the oldest dorm rooms of Yale, each with it own well used fireplace. Weekly, he received a grade on his demeanor and knowledge, to thin the ranks. Hyman survived and he was graduated to second lieutenant rank. He was assigned to an air base near his home for a short time and then to embarkation on the West Coast. After the ship departed he was informed his first assignment was Brisbane, Australia. Two days before arrival the ship received further orders -diversion to New Guinea. There he served in Finschhaven and Hollandia. As the action moved northward his posting followed the action. When the atom bombs were dropped on Japan he was in war torn Manila.

Ultimately discharged he returned to Baltimore to find his father's health seriously impaired. His fathers' doctor ordered immediate retirement. The following day Hyman took over the duties of running the family business.

For several years he made frequent trips to New York for buying. Thereafter his trips were to foreign countries purchasing hand made women's clothing accessories. His new sources were all in economically depressed countries, anywhere in the world.

He made these six weeks trips yearly, later semi-annually and soon set up travel programs of air travel weekends, working during the week. He found himself with open times between appointments. He kept himself busy with long walks to observe the country, the people, and their culture. Eventually all buying trips engendered a round the world ticket with frequent stops.

This proceeded for thirty-eight years until a growing trend in marketing made successful continuation of his business plan impossible. His customers originally were the small main street stores in the small towns of the U.S.A. With the dominance of chain stores, large shopping centers and department store consolidations his current volume customers were now buying directly from his own suppliers.

To avert a disaster he liquidated his business, paid off his creditors, and replanned his future. Although a senior he was mentally and physically still in a young condition. He needed stimulating work.

He decided to start over. It took a year but he finally found what he was looking for.

It was a service business that required no long distance traveling; didn't compete with foreign manufacturing and had a growth potential. The name of the prospective buy- "Global Messenger." A purchasing corporation was formed of Hyman's family - Paulyne his wife, to be principal owner and president, Steve - his son, to be Vice President and Hyman to be C.F.O.

At this stage of his life, Hyman was finding he was rising very early each morning. He used the extra time to read, to do personal book-keeping, working-out and reviewing notes of his earlier years while world traveling. All this led to an organizing of previous thoughts and their inscription onto paper, years passed. One day it suddenly occurred to Hyman that he had created the body of a book.. He named it I.O..-I.O. . Intuition, Observation, Imagination, Opinion.

www.ingramcontent.com/pod-product-compliance
Lightning Source LLC
Chambersburg PA
CBHW020307290526
45784CB00003B/1400